PUEDO SER PRESIDENTE/ I CAN BE THE PRESIDENT

By Alex Appleby   Traducido por Eida de la Vega

Gareth Stevens
PUBLISHING

Please visit our website, www.garethstevens.com. For a free color catalog of all our high-quality books, call toll free 1-800-542-2595 or fax 1-877-542-2596.

Library of Congress Cataloging-in-Publication Data

Appleby, Alex.
I can be the president = Puedo ser presidente / by Alex Appleby.
p. cm. – (When I grow up = Cuando sea grande)
Parallel title: Cuando sea grande.
In English and Spanish.
Includes index.
ISBN 978-1-4824-0867-6 (library binding)
1. Presidents – United States – Juvenile literature. I. Appleby, Alex. II. Title.
JK517.A66 2015
352.23–d23

First Edition

Published in 2015 by
Gareth Stevens Publishing
111 East 14th Street, Suite 349
New York, NY 10003

Editor: Ryan Nagelhout
Designer: Sarah Liddell
Spanish Translation: Eida de la Vega

Photo credits: Cover, p. 1 (girl) © iStockphoto.com/pkline; cover, p. 1 (White House) spirit of america/ Shutterstock.com; p. 5 S-F/Shutterstock.com; pp. 7, 24 (White House) Vacclav/Shutterstock.com; p. 9 Alex Wong/Staff/Getty Images News/Getty Images; p. 11 Barry Winiker/Photolibrary/Getty Images; p. 13 Joseph H. Bailey/National Geographic/Getty Images; p. 15 Eric Thayer/Getty Images News/Getty Images; p. 17 Peter Macdiarmid/Staff/Getty Images News/Getty Images; p. 19 Win McNamee/Staff/Getty Images News/Getty Images;
p. 21 JEWEL SAMAD/Staff/AFP/Getty Images; pp. 23, 24 (plane) EPG_EuroPhotoGraphics/Shutterstock.com.

Printed in the United States of America

CPSIA compliance information: Batch #CS15GS: For further information contact Gareth Stevens, New York, New York at 1-800-542-2595.

Contenido

- -

Contents

Quiero ser presidente.

I want to be president.

El presidente vive
en una casa grande.
Se llama
la Casa Blanca.

Presidents live
in a big house.
It is called
the White House.

Tiene muchas
habitaciones.

- -

It has many rooms.

¡Me gusta
el Cuarto Azul!

I love the Blue Room!

También tiene
un jardín grande.

It also has
a large garden.

13

El presidente saluda
a muchas personas.

Presidents meet
many people.

15

Se reune con
líderes importantes.

Some are
important leaders.

17

Y conoce
a artistas famosos.

Others are big stars!

La oficina del presidente es grande.
Se llama
la Oficina Oval.

Presidents work
in a big office.
This is the Oval Office.

¡Tiene su propio avión!
Se llama
Air Force One.

They have
their own plane!
It is called
Air Force One.

Palabras que debes saber/ Words to Know

(el) avión/ plane

(la) Casa Blanca/ White House

Índice/Index

24